ELIZABETHAN

XI

JONATHAN LOVEJOY

Jonathan Lovejoy

ELIZABETHAN

The Complete Poems of Elizabeth Peele

Volume XI

Jonathan Lovejoy

Cover: *Youth and Cupid,* 1877
William Adolph Bouguereau (1825-1905)

ISBN-10: 0692355499
ISBN-13: 978-0692355497

For every Elizabeth

Introduction

Carmen Angelina Coletti (Elizabeth Peele) was perhaps the greatest composer who ever lived. After her death, studies of her music revealed a body of work—almost exclusively instrumental—of such beauty and power as to defy description. Even so, her lifelong reclusiveness rendered them obsolete to the world, and these musical treasures may remain apart from public view forever.

Even those few who heard her original scores did so in quiet apprehension, that this beautiful widow—lost somewhere deep in North Carolina farming country—brought forth music as completely ingenious as any ever written before. The sounds of greatness flowing from this woman's piano, surely this is not meant to be! For what purpose can she truly serve as a neoclassical composer in a jaded modern world, except as a curiosity and eventually, a fountain of eternal exploitation?

But while music did serve as a profession for her since she was twelve—her only wage being a sound mind and spirit—there was still another expression, both private and unintentional, equally meant for her eyes only. Gathered posthumously, so few of these "assemblies" can be called unique or special, and likely cannot set her apart from any other lonely poet in the world. But still they live on, as a glimpse into the mind of a musical genius and abused woman of Faith. Written parallel to her music over the years—with no striving for greatness or immortality—these poetic trifles, ironically, may be the only compositions of hers the world will ever hear.

Jonathan Lovejoy

ELIZABETHAN

or

"The Assemblies"

Volume XI

Jonathan Lovejoy

Such is the grandest music among us—

Poets…

Such are the wildest thoughts among us—

Composers…

The Book of Emily

340th Assembly

1502

A tyrannosaurus rex—

Outside my window.

1503

*I*f I can heal one broken heart

Or ease a soul in pain

Just as She who cried before me

I shall not die in vain

If I see the fainting robin

"Unto his nest again..."

I shall not die in vain

1504

I won! The sentiment in the cold

Is there any pallbearer in the snow?

At what cost is the victory—

Written in the snow?

341st Assembly

1505

A train goes speeding off the tracks

Flying through the air

Though every life is jeopardy

Expectations fly

Praises—from the mouths of the dead

High into the air

As the train comes down a mile away

Upon the tracks

O Heavenly Father!

Save us from our Peril!

When the train goes speeding off the tracks—

Flying through the air--again.

1506

At the dinner after the train
The ancestry smiles.
Cake and meat for sustenance—
Reluctantly given.

1507

A teenager's self esteem

Is as brittle as glass.

Protected.

Never attacked—

By love.

1508

A gathering at the table
For business to attune
Making plans as we are able
Underneath the Summer Moon

Having no hope for tomorrow
We hum a dreary tune
Crushed under a hill of sorrow
Underneath the Summer Moon

In broken hearted affection
Lost in the afternoon
False Hope beckons resurrection
Underneath the Summer Moon

Jonathan Lovejoy

342nd Assembly

1509

A waving flag in the breeze
Lesbianism—for some
Traveling the highway to heaven
A prisoner of earthen needs

Greed stockpiles revulsion
Impulsively
Compulsion is the fever of life
In the jet propulsion age

The world stage is corrupted by sweat
The toil of human regret
Let the sunset happen, Fred—
Soon—you will be dead!

Lead is the Dead Man's Gold
Future heartache and pain
From the mountains to the shore of every sea
Above the fruited plain

1510

*D*eath said she was going to die

But she said, "No."

Covering her ears—

She walked away.

1511

Music played from another world
Unexplored on the earthen plane
Thunder for Carmen's orchestra
Lightning for her piano key

A storm of genius never wrought
Which no concert hall can contain
Fit for the angels in the night
To drown the Earth like Summer Rain

Born beneath the stars of Heaven
Screamed in summer's cricket song
Genius for piano and orchestra
To usher the end of the age along

1512

*H*aving elaborately refused—

Her nastiness is next

Jonathan Lovejoy

343rd Assembly

1513

At the low end of life—
A gate to comprehend
"Its not good English," she said
In days before the prairie plain—
And mountains on the horizon

1514

In the first hour after midnight

A shower's brief delight

Borne witness by two stars above

Between the clouds in flight

Over the nighttime woods adrift

To give thine perfect gift

A rain to ease a solemn heart

And dying curses to lift

1515

*T*he fire is hot—back off a bit

Except you may get burned

To hire or not--to call it quits

A lesson to be learned

Give what you've got—don't have a fit

Harvest what you have earned

Pain marks the spot—life takes a hit

Pray 'til the last hour is turned

A melting pot ain't worth a spit

If no one is concerned

Scribble a jot and tittle a wit—

Work 'til the butter is churned

1516

In the Land of Nighttime Delusion—
Lightning strikes!
Money troubles are the curse of God
Sent to plague a happy home

He comes as a thief in the night—
To steal prosperity away
A storm of false prosperity blows--
In Debt World

Lightning shows Nighttime Delusion
To expose the path of the thief
Seven hundred dollars is in the jeans—
With the hole in the pocket

Jonathan Lovejoy

344th Assembly

1517

On a jet plane ride to nowhere

Above the open sea

Water to every horizon

Beyond where I can see

Lost souls at the edge of torment

As much as they could tell

Their destination unawares

The fiery pits of Hell

All aboard the passenger plane!

Across the deep blue sea

Our destination unawares

If not for Calvary

1518

*F*rom the bowels of the Dead Room

Executes a mighty flight

From the Chamber of No Tomorrow

Along the Current of No Hope

New cloth covers the stench of death

For one of those in flight

Too stupid to kick and scream

Over the plane's destination

Understanding only water

Of the deep blue ocean sea

Knowing nothing of flames—

And the boiling ocean of fire

1519

*S*weet nothings are a feast

For ears to devour

Irrevalent—to say the least

In this—our final hour

Shoot the baskets—tow the line

When daytime turns to night

Corpses in the water must take a bow

For their insistence on living

Heroes are a reservoir—

Of self esteem to lend

Lean on them for a harvest yield

Before the age comes to end

1520

Unfit to receive the beautiful bride

Inside the Golden Palace

Cloth imbued as the skies above

Ocean eyes of blue

Jonathan Lovejoy

345th Assembly

1521

Creation spins another sun
Towards the evening day
Trees proclaim a vicious sunset
A wayward flock in flight

Shadows dancing long and heavy
Waked in Apollo's wheel
Amber fades to crimson bands—
Before the burial

1522

A connection divinely severed
In the bloodline of sin
Align thyselves with perfection
Carnality—to avoid

Rather to stay the Golden Road
From here to Prosperity
Though the queen seeks to abandon thee
On the road to Poverty

Unbeknownst—a lonely heart reaches out
For another soul in need
A divinely appointed connection
Of Carnality

Divinely anointed protection—
From Carnality

1523

There are no colors at night

All is dark'ned silhouette

'Cept the glow of man's light

Unnatural regret

1524

Where clouds go by unseen

A flash of silvery white

First quarter light of the Prairie Moon

By clouds unerring flight

346th Assembly

1525

Mountain shadows in the sky—
Devour thy Lunar Light!
Whispered by the night wind—
A grieving soul's delight

1526

The glory of the Lord in starlight

Above my feeble sight

For thy solemn breeze to prophecy

Lost fight of the Prairie Moon

1527

Beneath the mountain of night
Clouds lose their intrepid fight
Reemerge Luna in crimson—
Bow down to Beauty's Might!

1528

Killed by clouds of war

Choked in summer spite

Glows resurrection after the sword

In the blood of Crimson White

Jonathan Lovejoy

347th Assembly

1529

The first quarter turns to blood

Beneath a fervent summer's night

Having conqured each mighty cloud

By the blood of Redemption

1530

A Viper hidden in the room
Tanning brown forest leaf Gaboon!
But needles poisoned, pit and doom—
Shall have no power soon!

Eli! The taninbrown remove!
No such comeuppance overdue
Thine prayer where unbeknownst behoove
Taninbrowns--one and two!

Your death lay covered unforeseen
When Midnight walked across the floor
A second Viper! In between
The covers where you slept before!

1531

Stronger than heaven and earth

Was the bond they shared

To walk the earth as one

In sadness, sorrow and love

To roam the Earth in Creation

The grass--the leaves of every tree

Counterpose the color of Innocence—

Purity and spiritual Love

I see the color of Salvation

Strolling down the road

In bonded spirit with the unseen—

The Fury, the Rage, the depth of Anger.

Hidden.

In drops of rain—

The benevolent curse of God—

Bestowed upon the two of them.

For the children.

To see right from wrong
Good versus Evil.
To see righteousness from the clouds
In thunder and lightning

The wrath of the Almighty--
In the Storm.
To carry out Judgment over the wicked
To bring hope to a downtrodden soul.

Somewhere.

To roam the Earth in Creation
Power from on High
A storm of Purity
A deluge of Innocence
A maelstrom of spiritual Love.

Hidden.

A quick departure in the rain
To places unknown—
I see the benevolent Curse of God.
Walking alone.

1532

The skull with the hole in the top

Was definitely mine—

When the powder hath caressed through

Where my brain used to be

Of what importance was my life?

None but the curse of God

Perhaps, there is no need to morn

The inevitable

Do the hardest part of killing

Until the deed is done

A gift of brass and black powder—

For the pain in my head

348th Assembly

1533

The skull with the hole in the top
Was definitely mine—
When the powder hath caressed through
Where my brain used to be

Of what importance was my life?
None but the curse of God
Perhaps, there is no need to morn
The inevitable

Do the hardest part of killing
Until the deed is done
A gift of brass and black powder—
For the pain in my head

1534

From the clouds, I hear a nova!

A flaming nova—

Falling to Earth

1536

It will spread like a seed—

A corn seed

These are the stars that will grow

To the size of the universe

If this were but the course of events

A sign of the last days

A bright red circle in the night sky

Where a star used to be

1536

I saw the monsters move on Maple Street

Creatures of flesh and blood

Two legged—

Two armed—

Two eyed monsters—

On Maple Street.

In the course of human events

Thine comeuppance is overdue

When the monsters turn on one another

On Maple Street

Inevitably—

Irrefutably—

Undoubtedly—

Until someone dies—

When the bloodlust is through

The monsters were due.

On Maple Street.

Jonathan Lovejoy

349th Assembly

1537

There's money out there--

On them trees.

Its fun to take 'em--

If you please.

1538

I. *Serenity*

Cellos whisper a tune.
To prelude the approaching storm
To echo the approaching storm
Cellos whisper a tune.
Serenity when breezes form—
A melody in June.

By Summer's beating heart.
Before the cooling of the day
Before the clouding of the day
By Summer's beating heart.
Sunlight devoured in the gray--
By shadows fleeting heart.

Waves where green grasses flow.
Butterflies fluttering the wind
Bees and birds fluttering the wind
Waves where green grasses flow.
Harmony and peace know to end--
When stormy breezes blow.

Cellos whisper a tune.

In light of what deluge will come

In spite of what deluge will come

Cellos whisper a tune.

When thunder draws a breath to hum—

A melody in June.

II. Fury

Agitation falling in the wind—

A raindrop.

Agitation calling in the wind--

A raindrop.

Quivering the grassy prairie field—

A raindrop.

Shivering the grassy prairie field—

A raindrop.

Quivering the summer forest leaves—

A raindrop.

Shivering the summer forest leaves—

A raindrop.

A billion raindrops in the cloud—

A million raindrops in the air

Agitation pours a waterfall—tumbling through the air

Agitation soars a waterfall—rumbling through the air

A water mountain dropping down—to meet the wind below

A water mountain falling down—to greet the wind below—

SPLASH!

Thunder screams the skies!

CRASH!

Lightning screams arise!

FLASH!

Lightning shrieks demise!

When splashing thunder screams the skies!

SPLASHING water wall—drowning trees—droplets in the gust of eaves!

Leaves in breathless death to breathe—a billion splashes in the trees!

LIGHTNING splits the sky with ease--thunder shines the dreams of Eve!

Swirling wind--grassy plain--pray for a reprieve!

Wait! Embrace the energy charge—a *SPLASH* of lightning if you please!

Leaves of Grass—charred to soot

At the foot of the Judgment Throne!

Flames flickering in the rain—

Dying on the plain

Needles of pine—a solemn breath

Crying in the pain

Leaves of the prairie forest trees

Crying in the pain

Agitation falling in the wind—

Raindrops.

Quivering the grassy prairie field—

Raindrops.

Shivering the grassy prairie field—

Raindrops.

Quivering the forest leaves—

Raindrops.

Shivering the forest leaves—

Raindrops.

Raindrops.

Raindrops.

A raindrop.

A raindrop…

III. Beauty

Sunrise over the prairie green—

Over the prairie green.

Sunny wave in amber—

Over the prairie green.

Shine above the forest

Above the forest green

Ocean blue beams cotton white—

Above the forest green.

Morning sunrise belies the storm
Love lorned Beauty's summer warm
Morning skies in latter form
Over the prairie green

Morning sunshine belies the storm
Born in Beauty's summer warm
Morning skies in latter form
Above the forest green

Lilly whites and morningold
Yellow Rose's grief foretold
By petals snowy white
Near petal's red in brightest bold!
Violet's delight--behold!

Last morning's light in rightful pose
Last morning's might in right repose
Farewell, Dawn's early light!
Where these leaning petal grasses grow
Low down under weighted wind below
Kissed by what sweet valley breezes blow
Farewell, Dawn's early light!

Butterflies color night'n blue
Butterflies flutter white'n blue
Of leaning grasses green—

Rustled grasses in between
Where lads and lasses flew

Waving in the prairie wind
Of Beauty's timely end.
Of Beauty's timely end—portends
A waving in the wind—

Over the prairie green.

From mountain forest clearing fields
To the river valley green
Above the wooded forest grove
Over the prairie green

Sunshine above the forest grove
Over the prairie green
White doves alight the forest grove
Atop the prairie tree
Cooing doves in the forest grove
Over the prairie green

Sunshine over the prairie green
Where flowered grasses grow
Where sheaves by end time breezes flow
Over the prairie green.

Above the forest trees of life
Over the prairie green.
Ocean blue beams cotton white
Over the prairie green.

Sunrise climbing in the sky
Sunlight shining high.
Sunlight shining high.
Sunlight shining bye and bye—

Over the prairie green.

IV. Victory

Hark! A Lark!

A spark of Creativity!
A mark of the Nativity—

Hark—to hear!
The Lark is clear!

Embark to see the King of Kings
When mighty clouds of Judgment *reappear!*

To the dust, to the dust from where we came
To the dust, to the dust we go again

To the dust, to the dust from where we've been
To the dust, we'll go again

To the clay, to the clay we go again
To the clay, to the clay we know again
To the clay, to the clay we go and then
To the clay, we know again

The Redeemer comes in clouds of Heaven
Raise our bodies from the clay!
We will meet him in the clouds of Heaven
To escape the Judgment Day

The Redeemer comes in clouds of Glory
Save our bodies from the clay!
When we meet him in the clouds of Glory
We'll escape the Judgment Day

Signs and wonders have only begun
Signs and wonders—'til our age is done
Yet—

To the dust, to the dust from where we came
To the dust, to the dust we go again
To the dust, to the dust from where we've been
To the dust, we go again

To the clay, to the clay we go again
To the clay, to the clay we know again
To the clay, to the clay we go and then
To the clay, we know again

DEATH wields no power over me!
My heart and soul belong to Thee—
DEATH yields no pow'r over me!
My body and my mind to Thee—

There--is no grave to fear
There--is no coffin here
Though the cemetery marker does bear my name—
Though the marble at the cornice doth declare the same
There hath no effective lock for me—
Though the castle doth chamber my body to claim
There hath no effective lock and key

DEATH wields no power over me!
My body and my mind to Thee!
DEATH yields no pow'r over me
My heart and soul belong to Thee!

The Redeemer comes in clouds of Heaven
Raise our bodies from the clay!
We will meet him in the clouds of Heaven
To escape the Judgment Day!
The Redeemer comes in clouds of Glory

Raise our bodies from the clay!

When we meet Him in the clouds of Glory

We'll escape the Judgment Day!

Signs and wonders have only begun

Signs and wonders— 'til our age is done

Yet--

To the dust, to the dust from where we came

To the dust, to the dust we go again

To the dust, to the dust from where we've been

To the dust, we'll go again

To the sky, to the sky we look for Thee

To the sky, to the sky we call for thee!

To the sky, to the sky we long for Thee

To the sky, we—

BEHOLD! *Lightning* shines East to West!

Lightning shines from the East to the West!

My Saviour hath come to call me—

HOME!

The KING has come!

My LORD has come!

To call me HOME!

My Lord and Savior hath appeared

To raise our bodies from the clay that sought to--

BEHOLD! Lightning shineth East to West!
Lightning shineth from the East into the West!
My Lord and Savior hath called me--
HOME!
Upward we GO!
Into the CLOUDS!
To Him we GO!
To where we meet our LORD and SAVIOR
To be carried to a fair and distant--

Wait!

In the sky, in the sky we worship Him
In the sky, in the sky we sing our Joy
And our Praises to Him…

FIRE!

The WRATH OF GOD hath fallen to the evil
Left behind upon the Earth!
Pestilence, fire, earthquake, WHIRLWIND
War, famine, DEATH!

Redemption calls to save me
From the Wrath of Judgment Day!

To the dust from where I came--
From the dust--

To Paradise!

1539

*A*nd people say "*There is no God*"
What wonders hath ceased to fly?
To alight aft wings in flight—
Painted brown

Circles of beige and crimson
Spaced in symmetry?
As a flake of Summer snow—
Colored as the leaf in Autumn—
Born and raised in the Spring

1540

A set of bones in Christendom

Avenue of the dead

Gone the way of the dinosaur

Delusions to be fed

350th Assembly

1541

Beautiful trouble rides again

Eight legged symmetry

Fallen from the Tree of Good Hope

A fearful mystery

Monkeyshines in the Tree of Life

Deceit and Treachery

Betrayal in its purest form

Passive aggressively

In keeping with the luck I've known

And bitter history

Returning to the Tree of Hope—

Eight legged elegy

1542

Unstalled heavily in the snow

Steadily on the go

Epic wheels made ready to turn again

Don't you know!

We can work it out—

No need to scream and shout

Cracks may form in the region of space and time—

Reason to doubt!

But the ancestry sees the death of hope

Live! And learn to cope!

Hilary said—"*There's no need to keep beating a dead horse…*"

You misanthrope!

Jonathan Lovejoy

1543

Trouble blares a radio sound

Found outside my window

Lift my nerves into crescendo!

When trouble comes around

1544

Wave a dance in the breeze—

My lovely trees

Speak softly to the fence post bird

On future tragedies

1545

Envy covets thy neighbor's wife
And everything of his
Increased worldly goods and beauty
The best of all there is

Little girls running and playing
Their fenced in Summer's Eve
Offspringed by the God and Goddess
Of Good Luck to achieve

Envy covets Brangelina!
Brains and beauty galore!
Ruling their back yard paradise--
In Ardmore Village lore

King and Queen of Suburbia--
In Ardmore Village lore

351st Assembly

1546

Adultery is a non-issue

For them who understand

It brings with it the Curse of God

In waves upon the sand

Erode! Accursed foundation!

Where rocks were in the land

When lust—conceived and grown beneath

The blue of evening bands

1547

When I was a child in Williamston
The stars were brighter then
No city lights to interfere
As I remember when

After day had gone, night was night
As far as I could see
From the corner of my vision
The Sisters called to me

To hope for a joyful future
Under the cloak of night
Praying a prayer to every star
That twinkled in my sight

1548

As to this life I'm cursed to live

No good can come of it

Trapped like a cemetery ghost

My feet upon the grass

The barefoot rank is only best

To them it was desired

To them who sought the formal shoe—

T'is but a living death

1549

The end time streaks across the sky
Fireball of blue and white
To burn a warning through the night
That redemption draweth nigh

Cows graze the evening field
Turtles dive the fountain pool
Emblazened by the Aurora Comet
And fire from on High

352nd Assembly

1550

*T*he cake is ready!

Frost it in a pan!

Bring me some chocolate--

Icing in a can!

It don't matter who likes it

Its a confectionary plan!

Carried out by Destiny--

Outside the Will of Man!

The cake is ready!

Frosted in a pan!

Decorated chocolate--

Icing in a can!

1551

The white parchment under attack

By rock and dirt--and ashe and soot

Protected by a shelter unseen

In the midst of a dirty war

Born losers plant the seed

To cultivate a horizon tree

To watch it grow into a stifle

Choked of life and limb

Dogs are cooped on the bus of life

With half their faculties

But the white parchment glows with heaven's light

Shining from above

Goethe cannot crack the mainstream

Models say "you don't belong"

Hobble across the rock ground

In your quest to know the way

1552

From the gray clouds, stares the face of Beelzebub

A face so terrible—as to not be looked upon

In whose sight, carries no bravery or fear

But terror such as to dissipate the flesh

And penetrate the soul

The Eyes of Beelzebub look from the clouds

The Prince of the Powers of the Air

Ruler of the darkness of this world

In terrifying eyes that stare

1553

*W*hat divine mistreatment, there be

when *the blessing* is given to another

what divine mistreatment, I see

glazing the eyes of another

such a divine goddess, is she

enraptured by the face of another

what a divine goddess, there be

captured the world stage from another

such divine betrayal, there be

a promise deferred to another

what divine betrayal, I see

gazing

      the

        eyes

          of

353rd Assembly

1554

In the heart of memory, strolling through the field,
I see the leaves of the White Forest, calling to me.
Every leaf is as white as the petal of the rose,
To decorate the trunks of ivory wood.

And it seems that as I approach the forest of my youth,
And the trees of days long gone,
I can feel the grieving in every leaf and blossom,
Appearing as white as snow.

I stroll through the fields of green,
Away from the hidden house of gray,
Feeling the breeze across my face,
To dry the tears that threaten to flow.

When I stroll through the heart of memory,
I can see the place where the White Forest grows,
And I know that I must walk this journey,
To find where the petal of the crimson rose is grown.

In the forest,
Strolling the path to innocence,
Down the trail of my heart's desire,
The white leaves are a blanket beneath my feet.

High above me, from the tall trunks is the white leaf canopy,
Formed white as the clouds of Heaven.
This is Autumn of the White Woods,
When the leaves are subject to cool breezes that flow.

The breeze whirls the wooded alabaster trail,
And it blows my garment about me as a curtain in the wind,
Cloth born from the loom within,
A soul of melancholy blue.

My dress of the deepest blue midnight
Contrasts the ground of ivory white,
So that I am known as a creature fallen,
Who was cast down from days of purity.

I am innocence lost, strolling the heart of memory in midnight,
In the woods of winter white.

The breeze blows again, to lift my hair with my flowing cloth.
Leaves fall from the ivory wood,
Blowing down to where I stroll,
Falling like gigantic flakes of snow.

These are carried in this otherworldly breeze,

Until they whirl about me,

Taken on currents as the whirlwind,

Until I am among a swirling mass of white leaves,

Blowing in the wind.

I continue, hearing the tone of my piano in loneliness, calling me to fore.

But I do not go to it on this walk,

For I must complete my searching through the white woods,

To where I know the crimson petals grow…

While I feel pain and suffocation try as they might,

I breathe deeply this air of freedom,

And my eyes catch sight of my melody in question.

It is the single rose flower, on its lifeline made of white.

I hurry in the motion of the flowing wind,

And I retrieve the single red flower.

In the heart of memory,

I stroll the path through the White Forest,

To the place where love is crimson.

1555

The heat of righteousness is a flame
Burning blue and white fire
By the power of God blazing—
The Prophet's immortal soul

Though the bush burns righteous ire
From Genesis to Revelation
Times of confusion still linger
Like a summer morning fog

Catch a helicopter by the hand
Before it plunges to earth
The Power of God is a flame—
Burning blue and white fire

1556

It is better to dream from a distance

Than so steadfast and closely by

As to be burned

It is more delightful to dream

In Sanity's abode

Than to ride the nightmare train beside

Insanity's abode

1557

The dead man with the monster foot
Is dragged up from the grave
Looking to have his story told
Outside the loser's cave

Have a doughnut and don't worry!
The world's about to end!
Savour the dark with open arms—
Let Death become your friend!

The dead man has no appetite
Thanksgiving's gone away
Just two hops a skip and a jump—
Away from Judgment Day

1558

Cross the road and row to hoe—
A flock of problems to kill
Demons flow in from the highway
To babble more half truths and lies

Gray skies and blue skies and new skies to stay
Pay me my insult, before you go away!
Big problems to kill by chemical will?
Tell me something I don't know, Bill!

Demons grieve my time to rest
Obsessed to achieve my burial chest—
A million places to roam

The highway stretches a lonely road
Byways to go and hoe the row I'm owed
Along my journey home

354th Assembly

1559

Terror flowing in the breeze—
A scare! Rumbling a mighty wind!
Warning swishing in the trees
A bolt of lightning to descend

Demons haunt the darkened house
Ghosts stretch dreary arms to me
A cold breath—my skin to freeze—
Dancing darkness where I see

1560

Alone! No soul for company!

None to calm my heart of fear

Here--the voice of thunder, far and near

Two trees--with staring eyes to peer

1561

Atop the stairs! In the dark! Waiting for me!

No light to kill her bravery

An icy death by witchery

Found dead in my house alone

1562

The soothing dark after the storm
The pain of death is done
Resting well in my coffin bed
Rest where before there was none

Thunder rumbles my departure
Two trees watch over my grave
Wanting to speak of what they see--
Of the ghosts in my burial cave

Jonathan Lovejoy

355th Assembly

1563

*D*ark nights! Dark nights!
Imprisoned home alone
No one here to save me
From chills down to the bone

Shadows move—My sight! My sight!
Feeling what I see
Every creak and lonely moan
Reaching out to me

1564

Eyes adjust to the darkness
Where shadows go to rest
Staring down the silhouette
Is that where the shadow lives?

Lonely for my lifeline—
Pray thee, return to me!
But knowing I will die alone
With no one here to see

1565

Since no living soul could ever care

If Death should visit me—

Perhaps I should answer his fateful knock

And greet him willingly

356th Assembly

1566

Blue eyes playing in the dark—

Dancing down the road

Swaying with a purpose unknown

Where comeuppances are owed

Blue eyes glowing in the dark

Floating to and fro

Turning to notice where I am

When my lifeline is gone

1567

Now the rain begins again

To soothe a troubled soul

A song of night and tranquility

And coolness in the breeze

1568

The white chair on the black porch

Rocking in the dark

The white chair on the black porch

Is rocking

The white hand on the black door

Is knocking in the dark—

The white hand on the black door—

Is knocking

1569

The white chair on the black porch
Rocking in the dark
The white chair on the black porch
Is rocking

The white hand on the black door
Is knocking in the dark—
The white hand on the black door—
Is knocking

Jonathan Lovejoy

357th Assembly

1570

It looks like a giant boat

A giant canoe in the rain

Leaning the black forest silhouette

Waiting for rowers to come

Of what size and shape these rowers be—

Towers of treachery

Phased in from their ghostly world

To row their canoe away—

In the rain

1571

The level of fear is unknown
On the Professor's take
Its nigh time to draw a conclusion
Baked on the box of cake

Four years and a Grand Delusion
Does not a lifetime make
Pierce the heart of this illusion—
That pains my head to ache

John Hancock and a dead leaf prose
The newest bond to break—
Meant nothing and it never will—
My greatest dream mistake

1572

*F*lair will gouge my esteem with colored light.

While I wait for Emily to come home,
the evil of the Thriller beckons.
Michael Jackson's trial is a benchmark.
His very existence is a sign of the times.

After the war, a young man whose father is in the military has grown tired of bullying.
One day, he calls the three boys over to where he stands.
He slams one of the boys in the face with an empty paint can.
The boy's face needs stitches. It is a sign of the times.

A sixteen year old girl puts her diaphragm in, and has sex with her boyfriend.
The diaphragm was a gift from her mother on her sixteenth birthday--
it is a sign of the times. They are benchmarks, great and small,
along the road to our future.

Long after moonlight has faded, and night has turned to day.
Earthquakes, hurricanes, tornadoes, these are signs of the times.
The rise of comedy--the fall of tragedy.
The loss of love and respect for our fellow man.

The rule of Oprah Winfrey, the glory of money and fame.

Signs of the times these all are, both one and the same.

Spielberg's symphonies of light and sound--orchestras played from the Western Gate.

The explosion of Mount St. Helens, the fall of the Berlin Wall of hate--

these are signs of the times.

The Declaration of Independence. The Chorus of the Slaves,

the bloody Civil War itself--the killing of the Man of Lean.

When segregation was abolished through the killing of their King--

these are signs of the times we are in.

The roaring seas, the ocean waves--the great ships sailing to and fro--

the explosion of knowledge in the last 100 years. Our journeys into space.

The neverending tide of war and peace, the union of the European nations.

As the pirate ship rises from the east--burning blue and black fire,

these are signs of the times.

The Tri State Tornado of 1925, the 8,000 dead at Galveston Isle.

The National Football League--the writer of *The Green Mile*--

these are all signs that the end of the age is near.

The train of pearls on a string that slammed into the Jovian Sea--

the flight of Desperate Housewives from sea to shining sea.

Madame Rowling's wizard--the four children of Madame V.C.

These are all signs of the coming eschatology.

Jack and Rexella Van Impe. The life and death of Billy Graham.

The indescretion of Jimmy Swaggart, and President Clinton, I see.

When the arrows are flung from the desert east, and the towers implode poetically.

Theoretically, I see signs of the coming eschatology.

Rod Serling and his Twilight Zone--Theodore Geisel and his rhyme.

The posthumous life of Emily Dickinson. Longfellow's prose in time.

They are from the end of the age.

These are signs of the times.

Tonight, when Emily gets home, over an hour late from her curfew,

I'm going to fold one of her father's belts in front of her, as if it were going to happen.

I fold her father's belt, to see the sign of fear.

She tells me she is sorry. She is my daughter again.

My Emily's grave, I tend.

1573

In the forest of broken dreams

Trim Prosperity's lawn

We've got high hopes--we've got strong hopes—

Beyond the break of dawn

Two angels in the forest wood

Bring comfort as they should

For two lost in the wilderness—

At Ardmore Village Wood

Jonathan Lovejoy

358th Assembly

1574

Obstacles and discouragements
Cooked and served on a plate
Still wandering the grieving land
For freedom at the gate

Mothers and daughters gone awry
Asteroids on the way
Twelve year olds kill their mothers
Before the Judgment Day

Sisters burned by the mother's iron--
With nothing more to say

1575

Because of the grand scheme of things
He cannot get along
With no luck in his chosen life—
And nowhere else to go

"I'm in a new locale," he said
"A city by the sea—
The people here won't let me rest
From noise and partying"

"Where is it that you live, I asked—
The complex where you stay?"
"A place that shows erotic films—
24 hours a day..."

"A place of ill repute," I said
"Draws an unruly hoarde—
Get far away from where you live—
For righteous room and board"

Jonathan Lovejoy

1576

Eight legged battle to the death

When problems arise

My demise stalks the writing room—

In bitter poison

Lies inked in red truth

Across the white paper of life

Satan in brief disguise—

Hiding

1577

*T*oss around the black cloth—
Run it up the field
Spin and whirl your way through life
Until its all revealed

"You're a big mouth", mother says
In the curse of dirt and soot
Her face is twisted to a frown
Her compassion is gone kaput

"They're trying hard," sister says
I don't know why they're poor
I don't care--I'm getting out—
Its too much to endure!

359th Assembly

1578

Listen to the whispering wind
Bear down grief upon the trees
To burden them in sorrow
Of future atrocities

Calamities upon the earth—
Such as was never known
Swish, lonely trees! Bear knowledge of the fire—
Ache for thine whispering wisdom shown!

1579

*R*iding up the winter trail—

Where the Overlook awaits

Spirits cruise a watery wail

Flowing in the snow

The hotel lights are burning

Beckoning a call

At the edge of the atramental woods

Where snow begins to fall

Tony shows the bitter truth

Hiding in the cold

Streaks of red in the snowfall—

And ghostly men of old

1580

Prophecy on idols

Attached to the rear

Hear the song of the whistling bird—

Tweetering and twirtling here

A bat embraces the dark side—

Impact and beat the drums!

Evil is coming into the world

By a poisoned pen of fun

Just get ready—it's the end time

No need to wear a hat

You don't need one where you're going—

A Coronation is where its at!

1581

*F*ast forward—

Liquify.

Transmogrification—

Purify.

The details are in the steel

Melted on the line—

Dip a cup and drink it—

Its cemetery time!

Jonathan Lovejoy

360th Assembly

1582

A voice spoke softly through
Invitation in lavender
A yellow ticket to ride the train—
To a future unknown

Old friends deliver the word
In jealousy's repose
New friends joyful for what they've heard
Of a future in lavender

1583

These apart were restless—
Two—scattered in the wind
Like debris from a broken house
Shattered in the wind

1584

Pins and needles, needles and pins

Come to pierce my heart again

Bleeding on the new cloth

Hoping to remember when

1585

A gatherer awake in the cold—

Sorrow it to me

Let me hear the music of the chimes

In the Winds of Time

Among the trees and forest leaves

Melodies dance a tune

While Carmen wanders the wilderness tree—

Untouchable by me

Jonathan Lovejoy

361st Assembly

1586

When to kill a mockingbird
Is of utmost concern
Because of implications
And amenities to learn

Hearken the voice of Divinity
In the chimes of nature's song
Promises made by Him are kept
To mend a broken heart

Touch thine lips to revelation—
Awake! Ye muses nine!
Swear thine loyalty to mine—
Unwind her solemn twine!

1587

Sound the alarm bell—ringaling!
Do well to hear the tocsin ring
In the gloaming of the eve

Gather thy evening steps to roam—
Retrieve thy wayward daughter home
In hoping she will believe!

1588

In the song of the whispering wind

A devine melody

Spoken in the branches waving--

Heard by the grassy prairie field

Though the storm rages supreme--

Over the woods and field

A breath of renewal sings--

Above the sea of green

1589

A skeleton dipped in chocolate—
Is not a tasty meal
Except when it might be the bones—
Of a dead husband revealed

Creative Killings in a Coffin
Is the next evil thing
The bones of murdered women and men—
To accomp'ny the postman's ring

Jonathan Lovejoy

362nd Assembly

1590

Asleeping beauty lies pristine
Inside her forest tomb
Butterflies' curiosity—
Her hibernation womb

Rest--to sleep, but not death to keep
The trees and grassy room
Flowers such as were never seen
Reside her Harvest Loom

Her days upon the calender—
Awake! Thine beauty soon!
Loveliness sleeps the forest night—
Beneath the Harvest Moon

1591

Katie reports—*"she's a turkey!"*
A Dr. Pepper on her head
In the evening glow of city lights—
And the coming night to dread

John stares out the foggy window
Click a picture before you stop!
Mother-daughter perversion at the bottom—
Is the same as at the top

1592

Accused falsely of a drug deal—

In his native home alone

Carted off to the station—

Frozen to the bone

Suburban life of Paradise

Murdered by device

A friend's weed in the mailbox

Uncovered by The Vice

Cruising the wealthen stream

Along the land of plenty

Falsely accused of a drug deal—

For infinity

1593

Eyes crying in the dark—

Sarah.

Eyes.

Jonathan Lovejoy

363rd Assembly

1594

Asleeping tiger on the page

Flipped over on its back—

Fearful symmetry in deed—

No spirit left to bite

1595

Let us discuss our disgust—

With one another—

If we must.

Just dust after the rain

On a crust of clay

Robust feelings, I trust—

Are a gust of wind.

Lust and mistrust—

Won't hold us together

1596

The Music Man and the Man of Music
Appearing in the air
To sing songs in the Theatre of Life
With hardly a thought to care

Two comeuppances overdue—
At Golden Palace Station
One, abandoned by a nation—
The other--by inspiration

Both sent to tell me nothing—
In the theatre of broken dreams
Except that Hope is corrupted—
And Faith with works is dead

1597

Consider the birds of the air—
That neither toil nor spin
Protected in a mighty storm—
And rising gusts of wind

While the trees dip and sway
And swish and turn in the breeze—p
The birds close their eyes and pray
To set their hearts at ease

Jonathan Lovejoy

364th Assembly

1598

Amanda Peete wore black stockings--on her way home from school
Contrasted by the winter snow--there walks the Golden Rule
Lydia waits for her at home on Edgecombe County line
Tending her meal atop the stove—and to her sips of wine—

Take me home, Amanda Peete!
Thine coffin suite—Divine!

The stress of single motherhood--a daughter's mouth to feed
Dreams and a buried scream to whine—a longing to be free
To feel her when you close your eyes, underneath winter skies
Demise footprints the winter snow, with nowhere else to go—

Take me home, Amanda Peete!
Thine coffin suite—Divine!

What Fate? Thy darkest Destiny—at Edgecombe County line
Open the door and warm thy bones, her hearty sips of wine
A blast of yelling through the snow—a theatre of pain
Lydia screams *"Why were you late!"* Amanda screams in vain

Take me home, Amanda Peete—
Thine coffin suite--Divine!

Tears and blood in the House of White, At Edgecombe County line
Winter's Day into Winter's Night, and be not drunk with wine
One, encased by a coughing fit--the other's grief sublime
Every cough is another nail in Lydia's decline

"If you cough one more time!" she says—

In kind, coughs designed for muffling, behind her daughter's hand
Lifted Lydia from her bed, a hairbrush from the stand—
To march the evening flow—
Moving fast to Amanda's room, with nowhere left to go—
Her daughter lay face down to cough—her pillow white as snow

Then suddenly, she couldn't move, her world faded to black
A breath lost inside the pillow, a weight pressed on her back
From in the dark burned acid fire, her legs down to her feet
In grieving for a single breath—Death for Amanda Peete

Take me home, Amanda Peete
Thine coffin suite, Divine!

Lydia sat quiet and still—her life's mission complete
Agonized by regret and love, where two in twain shall meet
Until the body phased to cold—frozen eternal sleep
She prayed both their immortal souls—and Destiny to keep

She left her daughter there alone—
In night of Winter's deep

There lies two newly markered graves—the snow beneath the pine
Scalded skin and a smothered breath—pills and a glass of wine
Rest well, mother and daughter! Take solace in the snow—
There were no more prayers left to pray--and nowhere left to go

Tears and blood in the House of White
At Edgecome County line
Take me home, Amanda Peete—
Thine Palace Suite—Divine!

1599

In Spirit's lonely house—
I see the cool evening flow
Phased inadequacy in—
From Ghostworld into this

Ordinariness to nothing
The place the Ghost was in
But on this side of the astral curve
Extraordinary again

1600

Fifteen minutes to poverty

Is a heartbeat away

Except your plan to fame and fortune

Be devised by Him

Both failure and success

Are desperate in deed

In a fervor to show themselves

Somewhere along the way

Try as you might--no matter the fight

No need to try and win

When Victory is meant for thee--

She finds her own way in

1601

Poverty rises from the grave

To curse a happy home

The pink is back in the poultry—
My fears are coming back
It got this way because of sin—
And other things you lack

Poverty rises from the grave
To curse a happy home

Jonathan Lovejoy

322nd Assembly

1602

*T*ake me to Heaven when I die—O Lord!

Take me to Heaven when I die

Above these night woods—

Beyond the sky—

Take me to Heaven when I die

Lift me from this mortal sin

From this tormented flesh I'm in

Save me from misery and pain, O Lord—

Take me to Heaven when I die

Help me once more to breathe, Precious Lord

Bless me one breath of joy—

Employ thine angels to comfort me, Father—

That I can know happiness again

Beyond this night sky, I see

My Love and Redemption draweth nigh—

Take me to Heaven when I die, O Lord

Take me to Heaven when I die

1603

Won't "ocean" to others—
Some are oceaned by them
Slip, sliding away—
Back to where funtown is

To live and let live
Is the bomb to drop
By a heavenly kiss

Eagles--mountain nests
Above the prairie plain
Rising high over prosperity
Where Queen Elizabeth will reign

1604

With regret and apology—
I bid farewell to clarity
Words chosen by Him

Antlers turn to face—music
Slip—slide—away
Letters, syllables, syntax—
Rhyme or no rhythm
Rhythm or no rhyme

365th Assembly

1605

Pigs in a blanket—

Cared for by hogs

Hell without Christ.

1606

The rabbit jumped off the wagon

Run Harold, run!

Your day in the sun—

Unlucky rabbit's foot

Lois arranged her—

She's 25.

1607

*F*emale that biggest poetry anyway—
And receive her.

Yankee Doodle.

1608

Squealing pigs are the deal—
A meal.
Conceal yourself from the realness—
Less wordly.

Jonathan Lovejoy

366th Assembly

1609

Chris and Elizabeth carry the Word

The greatest composer who ever lived

Antonio Amadeus was she—

Mozart spun into Rossini—

And back again.

With modernity—

Music such as was never heard—

Along the timeline

To demonstrate the Power of God—

On Earth.

1610

*Y*ou're beautiful, comfortable—
Incredible, you're wonderful
Loveable doesn't describe you—
Huggable.

1611

Missed opportunity is a shadow

No substance--only illusion

For if it be missed--

T'was no opportunity to begin with!

ABOUT THE AUTHOR

Jonathan Lovejoy is a graduate of the University of North Carolina at Greensboro with a B.A. in Religious Studies, and a graduate of Liberty University with an M.A. in Theological Studies. He currently lives in Winston Salem, North Carolina.

For more info on the author's life and career, visit jonathanlovejoy.com.

www.ingramcontent.com/pod-product-compliance
Lightning Source LLC
Chambersburg PA
CBHW060924040426
42445CB00011B/780